Living and Nonliving in the Polar Regions

Rebecca Rissman

Heinemann
LIBRARY
Chicago, Illinois

© 2014 Heinemann Library
an imprint of Capstone Global Library, LLC
Chicago, Illinois

To contact Capstone Global Library please phone
800-747-4992, or visit our website
www.capstonepub.com

Edited by Daniel Nunn, Rebecca Rissman, and Catherine Veitch
Designed by Cynthia Della-Rovere
Picture research by Tracy Cummins
Production by Sophia Argyris
Originated by Capstone Global Library Ltd

ISBN 978-1-4109-5383-4 (hc)
ISBN 978-1-4109-5390-2 (pb)

Library of Congress Cataloging-in-Publication Data
Rissman, Rebecca.
  Living and nonliving in the polar regions / Rebecca Rissman.
      pages cm.—(Is it living or nonliving?)
  Includes bibliographical references and index.
  ISBN 978-1-4109-5383-4 (hb)—ISBN 978-1-4109-5390-2 (pb) 1. Natural history—Polar regions—Juvenile literature. 2. Life (Biology)—Juvenile literature. I. Title.

QH84.1.R576 2013
580—dc23   2012046871

Image Credits
Getty Images: DmitryND, 22; Minden Pictures: Flip Nicklin, 16, 17, 23, Yva Momatiuk and John Eastcott, 10; Shutterstock: BMJ, 7, Bronwyn Photo, 8, Bruce Rolff, 4, 23, Christopher Wood, 1, 6, 23, dalish, 13, Eirik Johan Solheim, 15, Galyna Andrushko, 23 (bottom right), Gentoo Multimedia Ltd., 20, hallam creations, 5, Maksym Deliyergiyev, 12, 23, Patrick Poendl, 21, Virginija Valatkiene, back cover, 18, Volodymyr Goinyk, 9, 11, yui, 14, 23, zahradales, 19; SuperStock: Minden Pictures, cover

We would like to thank Michael Bright and Nancy Harris for their invaluable help in the preparation of this book.

Every effort has been made to contact copyright holders of material reproduced in this book. Any omissions will be rectified in subsequent printings if notice is given to the publisher.

All the Internet addresses (URLs) given in this book were valid at the time of going to press. However, due to the dynamic nature of the Internet, some addresses may have changed, or sites may have changed or ceased to exist since publication. While the author and publisher regret any inconvenience this may cause readers, no responsibility for any such changes can be accepted by either the author or the publisher.

Some words are in bold, **like this**.
You can find them in the glossary on page 23.

Printed in the United States   6078

Contents

What Are the Polar Regions?

The polar regions are areas on Earth that are very cold.

The polar regions are close to the **north** and **south poles**.

north pole

south pole

Different types of plants and animals live in the polar regions.

There are **nonliving** things in the polar regions too.

What Are Living Things?

Living things are alive. Living things need air and **sunlight**. Living things need food and water.

Living things move on their own.

Living things grow and change.

What Are Nonliving Things?

Nonliving things are not alive. Nonliving things do not need air and **sunlight**.

Nonliving things do not need food and water.

Nonliving things do not grow and change on their own.

Nonliving things do not move on their own.

Is a Seal Living or Nonliving?

A seal needs food and water.

A seal moves on its own.

A seal grows and changes.

A seal needs air and **sunlight**.

A seal is **living**.

Is Lichen Living or Nonliving?

Lichen needs water.

Lichen moves on its own toward the sun.

Lichen grows and changes.

Lichen needs air and **sunlight**.

Lichen is **living**.

Is a Rock Living or Nonliving?

A rock does not grow on its own.

A rock does not need air or **sunlight**.

A rock does not need food or water.

A rock does not move on its own.

A rock is **nonliving**.

Is a Narwhal Living or Nonliving?

A **narwhal** grows and changes.

A narwhal needs food and water.

A narwhal needs air and **sunlight**.

A narwhal moves on its own.

A narwhal is **living**.

Is Ice Living or Nonliving?

Ice does not move on its own.

Ice does not need food.

Ice does not grow.

Ice does not need air or **sunlight**.

Ice is **nonliving**.

Is a Penguin Living or Nonliving?

A penguin grows and changes.

A penguin needs air and **sunlight**.

A penguin needs food and water.

A penguin moves on its own.

A penguin is **living**.

What Do You Think?

Is this fox **living** or **nonliving**?

Glossary

lichen
simple plant

north pole
the place
farthest north
on Earth

living alive. Living
things need food and
water. They breathe,
move on their own,
grow, and change.

south pole
the place
farthest south
on Earth

narwhal
type of whale

sunlight
light from
the sun

nonliving not alive.
Nonliving things do not need
food or water. They do not
move on their own, or grow
and change.

Find Out More

Websites

Facthound offers a safe, fun way to find Internet sites related to this book. All of the sites on Facthound have been researched by our staff.

Here's all you do:
Visit www.facthound.com
Type in this code: 9781410953834

Books

Lindeen, Carol K. *Living and Nonliving*. Mankato, Minn.: Capstone, 2008.

Marsico, Katie. *A Day in the Life: Polar Animals* (series). Chicago: Heinemann, 2012.

Waldron, Melanie. *Polar Regions (Habitat Survival)*. Chicago: Raintree, 2013.

Index